For my parents, Flora and Douglas Churnin,
with gratitude for bringing me up in a
world of books and love—NC

For Mama and Papa.
Thanks for believing in me.—JT

William scooped dust to dry the sweat off his slick rubber ball. He stared at the small *X* he'd chalked on the barn wall. He closed his eyes. He opened them and threw. Bam! He hit the mark. He stepped back so he could try again.

His mother waved her arms. She was applauding him.

She touched her fingers to her mouth to signal eating. He read her lips as she said, "Dinner."

William pulled out his pad and pencil. He scribbled: "Just a few more? I want to be perfect for tryouts."

His mother nodded.

His family was passing the mashed potatoes around the table when William pushed open the door. He read his father's lips telling him to wash up for dinner. He also read what his father's lips mouthed to his mother.

"Baseball," his father said, shaking his head. "It will never last."

Still, William couldn't wait to try out at his school, the Ohio State School for the Deaf. At tryouts, he threw the ball. He caught it. He batted. He waited.

"Too small," the team captain said.

William never got much taller than five-foot-five. He couldn't do anything about that.

But maybe they'd give him another chance if he aimed better and ran faster.

So every day, after homework and chores, he practiced.

One day William was standing outside the cobbler shop where he fixed shoes, wistfully watching men play baseball in a far-off field. A foul ball crashed by his feet. With his strong, sure arm, he threw the ball straight into an amazed player's waiting hand.

"Hey, kid," the player called. "Want to join us?"

But William couldn't read the player's lips from where he was. So he turned back to work.

The man ran to William and tapped his back to get his attention. William whirled around, and this time, when the man repeated the question, he understood. He scrambled happily to the outfield.

William threw the ball smack into his teammates' hands. When he was up at bat, he sent it soaring where no one could catch it.

"What's your name?" asked one of the players.

William Hoy, William wrote.

The man looked at the piece of paper a long time.
He seemed to be thinking.

"Do you want to try out for our team?" he asked
William at last.

William grinned. He sure did!

William soon learned life in the hearing world wasn't easy. Unlike his parents, few people used sign language in the 1880s, and certainly not in baseball. He won a spot on the first team he tried out for, but the manager smirked when he offered William less money than he paid the others.

"I quit," William told him with his notebook. He quickly found another team.

But even on his new team, some players talked behind
his back so he wouldn't know what they were saying.
Others hid their mouths so he couldn't read their lips.

One day a pitcher played the meanest trick of all. William let three pitches go by because he thought they were balls. He was too far to read the umpire's lips and didn't know they were actually strikes. He stood, gripping his bat, waiting for the next pitch. But the next pitch never came. William was confused. Suddenly the pitcher burst out laughing. He pointed to the fans in the stands laughing too.

William's face grew hot. He walked off quickly. He wasn't going to cry. Not about baseball, he told himself.

He jammed his hands in his pockets. Paper crunched against his fist. He pulled out a letter from his mother. He read again how much she missed him.

William missed his family too. He remembered how his mom would raise her arms to applaud him.

That's it! William pulled out his pad and drew pictures. He scribbled words next to the pictures. He wrote. He wrote. He WROTE! He ran to find the umpire.

The umpire read William's notes.
"Yes, that could work," he said.

The next time William was at bat, the umpire raised his right hand for a strike and his left for a ball.

He used American Sign Language symbols for safe and out. This time William got on base. He stole bases. He scored!

In his first year in the majors, he led the National League in stolen bases.

With his strong, sure arm, he became the first player to throw three base runners out at the plate in one game—from the outfield!

William taught his teammates signs so they could discuss plays without the other team hearing. They loved it!

The fans enjoyed learning signs too. In those days, before speakers and giant screens, hearing the umpire's calls from the back of the bleachers was hard to do! Now, even the farthest member of the crowd could see the signals.

Teams begged for William. He played for several before signing with the Cincinnati Reds, near his family's farm.

William was proud to show his parents that the boy who didn't make the school team was one of the most popular players in baseball.

When William stepped up to the plate,
shaking his bat over his shoulder,
fans knew he'd hit or walk his way to
first, then swiftly steal his way around
the bases.

Carefully watching the signals,
he led the American League in
walks in 1901. He was called
the king of center field because
for ten years he was ranked
among the top five outfielders
to get hitters out by catching
hard-to-reach fly balls.

After William became a star, he thought nothing could surprise him. Then, one day, when he ran out onto the field, fans waved their arms from the stands just as his mother did when he was a boy. They waved hats too.

William said he'd never cry about baseball. But he did cry at the sight of deaf applause. All he'd wanted to do since he was a boy was find a way to play his favorite game. He never dreamed he'd change how the game was played. But he did, and we still cheer him today.

MORE ABOUT WILLIAM HOY

When you look up William Ellsworth Hoy, you often find him referred to as Dummy Hoy. During William's time, Dummy was a common name for people who were deaf and mute. William, who was proud of being deaf, referred to himself as Dummy.

While William has long been a hero in the deaf community, he's not as well known in the hearing world, even though he broke many records and became one of baseball's most popular players from 1888–1902. He was born May 23, 1862, in Houcktown, Ohio, on his parents' farm. He was the only member of his family who was deaf; he had lost his hearing at a young age from meningitis. After William graduated as valedictorian of the Ohio State School for the Deaf in Columbus, Ohio, his parents hoped he'd settle down to a respectable life as a cobbler, but he loved baseball. He continued to fix shoes in between seasons.

William went all-out for every play. Once he jumped onto a horse standing on the edge of the outfield just to catch a ball.

He also had a sense of humor. When his team had been kept up all night by loud guests at a hotel, William bragged about how well rested he was because he was deaf.

William Hoy was not the only person to introduce hand signals to the game, but he did work with umpires to develop a number of signs he would need to succeed before signals became official in baseball.

He married Anna Maria Lowry, a teacher of the deaf who was deaf herself, and they raised their children and a nephew on a dairy farm near Mount Healthy, Ohio. After retiring from baseball, he worked as a personnel director for the Goodyear Company and organized the company's deaf workers into a baseball team he called the Goodyear Silents.

William received a standing ovation when he threw the first pitch before Game 3 of the 1961 World Series when the Cincinnati Reds played the New York Yankees. He was ninety-nine years old.

In the years since his death, William Hoy has been inducted into numerous baseball halls of fame: the Hancock Sports Hall of Fame in 1989; the Ohio State School for the Deaf Hall of Fame in 1990; the Ohio Baseball Hall of Fame in 1992; the Cincinnati Reds Hall of Fame in 2003, and the Baseball Reliquary Shrine of the Eternals in 2004.

TIMELINE

WASHINGTON

WILLIAM HOY

1862 William Ellsworth Hoy is born on May 23 in Houcktown, Ohio, during the presidency of Abraham Lincoln.

1865 William contracts meningitis and loses his hearing and speech.

1879 Graduates as valedictorian from the Ohio School for the Deaf. Repairs shoes in Houcktown and continues to practice baseball.

1886–1887 Signs his first professional baseball contract with a minor league team in Oshkosh, Wisconsin.

1888–1889 Sets National League record for stolen bases in his major league rookie year with the Washington Nationals. In his second year, he throws out three runners at home plate in one game from the outfield.

1890–1901 Plays for Buffalo Bisons, St. Louis Browns, Washington Senators, Cincinnati Reds, Louisville Colonels, Chicago White Stockings (which eventually become the Chicago White Sox).

1901 Hits grand slam for Chicago White Stockings against the Detroit Tigers to help his team win the American pennant.

1902 While playing for the Cincinnati Reds, Hoy gets a walk off of deaf pitcher Luther "Dummy" Taylor of the New York Giants. It was the first time in major league history that two deaf players faced one another in a game.

1941 Inducted into Louisville Colonels Hall of Fame.

1951 First person inducted into the American Athletic Association of the Deaf Hall of Fame.

1961 Throws first pitch during Game 3 of the World Series between the Cincinnati Reds and the New York Yankees. Dies December 15 at age ninety-nine during presidency of John F. Kennedy.

Full name:
William Ellsworth Hoy

Nicknames: Will, Dummy Hoy

Hometown: Houcktown, Ohio

Birthdate: May 23, 1862

Height: 5'5"

Weight: 148 pounds

Bats: Left-handed

Throws: Right-handed

Teams: Washington Nationals (1888–1889); Buffalo Bisons (1890); St. Louis Browns (1891); Washington Senators (1892–1893); Cincinnati Reds (1894–1897); Louisville Colonels (1898–1899); Chicago White Sox (1901); Cincinnati Reds (1902)